Cake Decorating

The Ultimate Guide to Mastering Cake Decorating for Beginners in 30 Minutes or Less!

Copyright © 2015

Table of Contents

Introduction

First and foremost I want to thank you for downloading the book, "Cake Decorating: The Ultimate Guide to Mastering Cake Decorating for Beginners in 30 Minutes or Less!"

In this book you will learn how to decorate your own cake for festive occasions. Moreover, this book is aimed for beginners like you with its step-by-step process of cake decoration. Once you mastered these fundamental techniques, you will eventually enhance your skills by experimenting and incorporating your own ideas.

For those who are fond of baking and want to make their cakes more pleasing to the eye, we got you basic and inexpensive ways on how you can decorate your cake easily. From melting chocolate bars to shop-bought icing and fondant, you can create a masterpiece with our handy tips.

Furthermore, making your cake look impressive and professional do not have to expensive and difficult as what most of us assume. Here we will provide you easy techniques that you can try at your own home.

Feel free to try these decorating ideas for special occasions and events while enhancing your baking skills at the same time.

Thanks again for downloading this book, I hope you enjoy it!

Chapter 1

Our Love for Homemade Cakes

Almost all of us love cake especially in celebrating milestones and events in our life. However, homemade cakes are most special since it comes with effort, time spent, feeling and appreciation. It is a greater expression of gratitude and love compared to purchase ones from the store.

Although the cake is only homemade, it doesn't have to be plain and less appealing compared to cakes created by professional pastry chefs. Upon learning the basics, you will also learn in this book various icing types and other cake decorating tips.

The Making of a Cake

So anybody can make a cake however, it is an art to come up with a cake that won't crumble or collapse all over. The cake is the actual canvass and its surface is where you will be creating your art hence, your cake should be icing-friendly. Moreover, your cake should not have crispy edges or is tilted to a certain side or you will find it difficult to roll fondant and put other decorations. Another thing is the shape of the pans to use. Make sure to only use pans that are in good condition to avoid wasting cakes and spending more time in cutting and leveling the cake.

Start with a quality pan

Preheat the oven according to the temperature stated in your cake recipe

Polish the pan with solid vegetable shortening. Avoid using margarine, butter and other liquid based vegetable oils. This will only turn your cake to have crisp edges and burns. It can also stick to the pan.

Lightly dust the pan with flour ensuring that you cover all the greased surfaces. Dust it again if you see some shiny spots. If you want to skip the dusting and larding part, you can use products that can make the cake easily pop.

Pour the batter in the pan; evenly spread the batter using a spatula. After that, bake your cake in the preheated oven depending the time indicated in the cake recipe.

If you don't have a cake tester, you can use a toothpick to test if your cake is well done. If the tip comes clean after removing it, then it is done but if the batter is still visible, bake the cake for a few more minutes and repeat the test.

Remove the cake from the oven let it cool in the pan for about 10 minutes. Flip the cake over a cooling rack to unmold it. Carefully lift the pan and brush the loose crumbs gently.

How to Level the Cake

Your cake won't be straight and flat without leveling it. Leveling basically mean removing any bumps or crown from the cake making it an even surface where you can easily decorate. If you don't have a cake leveler, a kitchen knife will do.

Usually, cake levelers come in different notches where you will insert wires to torte the cake (separate it in layers). It also comes in several sizes to suit the cake. To lever the cake, put it in a cake cardboard and measure the height to cut from it. Position the cutting wire's ends to the side notches and cut it with an easy slide.

If you are using a knife, place the cake in a turntable. Slowly rotate it while moving the knife back and forth (sawing motion) to remove the crown. Keep the knife level as possible while cutting the cake then brush slowly the loose crumbs. If working with two or three-tier cake, start decorating from the top and work your way to the bottom.

It's normal for a newbie like you to get excited and may desire to jump straight in making three-tier masterpiece however, it will only bring frustrations so start with little steps. Prefect a crumb coated buttercream cake first then try doing it with some fondant ribbon roses and so on.

Master the simple and basic techniques first before learning more complex decor. Take time as cake decorating is a process that requires your patience, focus and labor of love. Likewise, baking your cake properly is as important as decorating it. You will get to know more of these techniques and tips as we discussed various elements of cake decorations.

Chapter 2

Putting Some Icing

To become successful in decorating your cake, you must have that overall look in your head even before you start. You can get ideas from other cakes in a bake shop nearby or in food-related or events magazines. This will make it easier for you to decide what to use in decorating.

While it is the decoration that catches our interest when it comes to cakes, the most crucial thing for a perfect cake decoration is the icing. When the consistency of the icing is not right, more likely that your decorations will not also be right. A very small amount of liquid can have a significant on the icing's consistency and so as with your decorations. Factors such as ingredients, temperature, humidity and equipment may also affect it. Likewise you have to work with various icing consistencies when decorating.

The Icing to Your Cake

Icing a cake can be tricky especially if you also have to keep the crumbs out of it. The trick is to make the first layer of icing thinner as you spread it on top. The first coat serves as the foundation layer, sealing the cake and preparing it for additional decorative moldings. Another tip is to make the first layer thin with small amount of corn syrup. This will prevent the cake from sticking. If you feel that the icing is thick than it should be, add a little liquid and if it's too thin, adding some confectioner's sugar will help.

Similarly, you can let the spatula glide on the surface of the cake but without touching the cake's top. There are plenty of ways on how you can dress up a homemade cake. Below are basic steps in icing the cake using butter cream royal icing;

1. Place a huge amount of icing in the cake's center but make sure that is consistently thin. Spread across the top of the cake's surface.

2. Push down on the sides the excess icing. Ice all the sides a section at a time. When all the sides are entirely covered, hold your spatula with its edge against the cake's side while slowly spinning the cake turntable. Do this without lifting your spatula from the surface.

3. Remove the excess icing and repeat the process until the sides are all smooth. Do the same process at the top of the cake until it is entirely covered with icing.

There you go! You already have a canvass cake that you can decorate with. You can use different types of icing for your decoration. Butter cream icing is popular especially to those who want to create realistic flowers and drapery on their cake. Basically, any icing will work including those ready-made that you can purchase at the stores.

Preparing the Decorating Bag

The next step is to assemble the decorating bag you will use. For beginners, a disposable plastic or parchment paper bag can suffice but it is also advisable to use decorating bags made of washable polyester.

Insert the **coupler** at the tip of the bag. You can buy one from department stores, home supplies shop and grocery stores. The coupler is important since it can keep the decorating details steady. It is also helpful in changing decorating tips. Select a decorating tip that has big, round opening then attach the coupler base. Put the ring back to the tip and screw it tightly.

Piping Icing

If you want to write dedications on the cake then piping icing is the best. You can also pipe some stars, hearts and other symbols to make the cake more appealing. Doing the same procedure of icing the cake, you can now proceed to piping. You will need pastry bags or plastic bags with couplers, different decorating tips, icing spatulas, cake turntable and food coloring for the icing. Choose gel-paste food coloring's over liquid coloring as it won't dissolve the buttercream and is more concentrated.

Assemble the pastry bag and coupler and your chosen tip. Fill the bag with icing using a spatula and scrape the excess icing on the sides of the bag. Remember not to fill the pastry bag more than halfway or you will find it difficult to hold it properly while piping. A small amount will allow you to get the hang of using it.

Gather the edges in one hand then use your index and thumb finger to push the icing downward until it reach the decorating tip. Before actually piping the cake, practice your strokes first on a parchment paper.

Different types of pastry bag tips can be used to come up with various looks and effect on your cake;

Star tips - can create flowers, stars, shells, rosettes and decorative borders

Round tips - perfect in creating dots and lines and writing messages

Leaf tips - great for leaf-like shapes

Basket-weave tips - used in making ribbon like shapes, lines and borders

Some Tricks:

- You can use a toothpick to sketch out letters and shapes into the surface of the cake. If you are not satisfied with the pattern, smooth the frosting over again using a spatula and try sketching again. Make sure to use minimal pressure while sketching.

- Cookie cutters are also helpful in creating designs. Neatly press a cookie cutter into the cake frosting then pipe over the imprints.

- Use a round tip to squeeze a thick icing on the top edge of the cake. This will serve as a border to avoid spilling the icing.

Add Some Fillings

After the entire edge of the cake was covered, you start filling in. aside from icing you can use pudding, custard, fruits or whipped cream. Start at the center and work your way out until the border. There are plenty of ingredients that you can use as fillings.

Chapter 3

Frostings, Glazes and Fillings

You can use a combination of techniques in decorating your cake. For example, a custard and syrup can be put in between the layers while you have frostings on the outside and other pipe decorations. However some of the techniques go well with a certain type of cake. Thus, mixing and matching of these finishing techniques will help you become more creative in making your cake appealing and appetizing at the same time.

In Between Fillings

The filling is usually in between the cake's layers or inside of it when rolled up. Many prefer their cakes to have more than one filling all together altering berries, whipped cream and buttercream. Below are some other popular fillings you can use.

Custards – includes pastry cream and fruits curds like orange and lemon curd, custards are popularly used in most European-style cakes such as genoise. Pastry creams can have vanilla flavors and some whipped cream. However custards are extremely rich so they usually have this wrong texture if used in covering the outside of the cake. You might try to use custards with cream cheese frosting instead to flavor the cake.

Whipped cream – this fluffy ingredient is a classic filling used I most cakes. It works well with flavored cakes and can also be paired with fruit fillings. Likewise whipped cream can be used in piping small details to your cake or to cover it.

Sugar syrup – this can be brushed on the layers of the cake to moisten it especially drier cakes. Syrup is also a staple in wedding cakes as it keeps the cake's freshness although it is several days old prior to serving. In general, syrups are used with buttercream or jam filling.

Jellies and jams – are also among the favorites and can be combined with other fillings such as fruits and buttercream. Make sure to strain the seeds however to smoothen the jam's texture.

Buttercream – is one versatile ingredient that can go along with oil and butter cakes and genoise-based cakes. It can also be used in piping decorations. The traditional buttercream uses eggs and sugar as a base added with soft butter. Flavorings were also added after including chocolate, fruit puree, coffee and meringues.

Ganache – is a rich mixture of cream and chocolate that you can pair with various types of cakes. You can also modify the richness by changing the ration of cream to chocolate. Putting more chocolate than cream will make the mixture thick which is good in filling cake layers.

Glazes

Sometimes glazes are used to varnish cakes before putting the icing. It originally comes from French pastry chefs as a way to preserve cakes. The glaze seals the cake from air and prevents it from drying. There are also various types of glaze you can choose from.

Chocolate glaze – chocolates are very versatile as ingredients for cake decoration. To make a rich chocolate glaze, add cocoa powder to simple glaze (a mixture of water and sugar). Others use milk instead of water to achieve a richer glaze. You can add maple syrup for extra flavor. For a caramel glaze, pour some brown sugar, water and butter in a pan and let it simmer.

Flavored glaze – you can add any flavored extract to your simple glaze but make sure that it complements your cake. Some prefer to add few drops of root beer, rum, banana, almond and amaretto to come up with a flavorful glaze. Savory spices such as basil and anise can also be used.

Learn to Cover-Up

Not all mediums such ad buttercream and fondant are perfect to use in cake decorating hence, you might make mistakes now and then. These mediums can be affected by humidity levels and weather. If you made a mistake that can no longer be fixed by adding more cream or fondant, cascade some polka dots, borders, flowers or candy to cover-up the mistakes. As you learn more techniques, you will soon improve your skills. Practice helps so keep on making those cakes and find your own technique and specialty.

Chapter 4

Yummy Elements to Try

Aside from the items we discussed above, there are other plenty of elements you can use to decorate the inside and out of your cake. Most of the cakes are decorated by molding or piping decorations and various mediums were used as fillings. Below are some of the most popular decorating mediums to choose from.

Water icing – this is made from water or milk and confectioner's sugar. You can add flavoring like vanilla extract or citrus juice to it. Coffee cake and pound cake can be brushed with thin water icing.

Rolled fondant – another favorite, rolled fondant is a combination of vegetable shortening and sugar. The mixture will make a puttylike substance that can be stretched or rolled like those of pastry dough. Rolled fondant is also one of the favorites of cake artists since it can be tinted with any food coloring, can hold up despite hot weather and forms smooth surface which is perfect for any decorations. However although fondant looks terrific, the cake will taste terrible if applied too thick.

Marzipan – is also a thick material that can be used to cover cakes however, this nutty almond paste is usually off-white in color and sweet so it is not quite good for tinting. Likewise, marzipan is typically used in molding flowers and small decoration placed on a cake.

Likewise marzipan is traditionally used in Christmas cakes. Just make sure that you don't warm it too much using your hands or it will sweat and becomes tricky to roll.

Royal icing – made from confectioner's sugar and a heavy paste of egg whites, beaten together with strained lemon juice or vinegar. This sticky icing is normally used in delicate piping. Likewise its pure-white finish makes it good for tinting. Although it is sweet, do not use it in large amounts as it tends to crisp when dry.

Royal icing also works best with Christmas themes since it is pure-white in color. You can color it as well using gel pastes. However, do not use liquid food coloring or it will alter the icing's consistency.

Melted chocolate- you can do many things with melted chocolates. It can be used to write dedications or drizzled as the cake's decoration. Dark chocolates look awesome with light-colored frosting.

Meringues – you can dress up your cake by using store-brought meringue. Put it around the edge of your cake as a crunchy alternative to rosettes. If it's your first time to make a meringue, try cooking it slowly on a low heat or in the oven and add it as a topping to your cake instead of spreading it.

Gum paste – can be created as edible and candy-like decorations. It can also serve as glue to adhere flowers and other small decorations onto the cake. You can also have it as a seam in fondant if you are adhering two slabs of fondant to cover the cake.

Other Food Ingredients

Chocolates and sweets – whether you cover the entire cake, or pile it in the middle, or spell the celebrator's name, chocolates and other sweets are best cake decorations especially for children. Before covering the cake with sweets and chocolates, make sure that you cover it first with melted chocolate coating or light buttercream so the sweets will not fall all over the cake.

Fruits – for those who want their cakes to be light and refreshing, fruits are highly recommended. Dried raisins, fresh berries, strawberries and other fruits would be the perfect topping for your cake. When using fresh fruits, add it at the last minute or place your cake in the fridge first before you actually consume it to preserve the fruits' freshness.

Nuts – we know for a fact that nuts are very healthy and incorporating it with your cake makes it more wonderful. You can sprinkle some nuts on top of the cake or cover the whole cake. It is best to match the nuts with the cake you are making. Peanuts or almonds are better with chocolate cake and walnuts complement carrot cake.

Cigarellos and chocolate fingers – got some flaws on your cake? Cigarellos and chocolate fingers are great techniques for that sweet cover-up. Just cover the affected area with buttercream, royal icing or chocolate then press the chocolate fingers or cigarellos around the edges. It is also a great base for sweet toppings, flowers and fruits.

Spreads – marmalade, peanut butter or Nutella, spreads are always a good choice especially if you are running out of time and budget to fully decorate your cake. Spread it evenly on top of the cake using a spoon or knife. Add some sprinkles, fresh fruits or fondant shapes. For thick spreads such as peanut butter and Nutella, slightly warm it to melt a little so it will be easier for you to spread.

Cream – whipped cream is usually used as bases for fruits, sprinkles and chocolates as it is easier to work with cream. However, make sure that you keep the whipped cream chilled for better consistency. When making a cake, make the cream first and leave it in the fridge and add it lastly to your cake.

For most of us, the idea of making our own cakes, decorating and frosting it seems overwhelming and difficult but it shouldn't be. You can get various ideas on how to make you cakes wonderful and extremely appealing to the eyes and taste buds. Create your own decoration using the ingredients above and mix and match new element that comes in your mind. If you are working with a theme, be sure to incorporate related designs and patterns to pull it up together.

Chapter 5

More Easy Cake Decor Ideas and Products

Decorating your cake can be done in a hundred of ways. Some techniques require skills and materials while some just need inexpensive food ingredients and a little creativity there. Fortunately the cake industry has been producing more creative products that can add a touch of uniqueness and originality to cakes. Here are some inspiring products on the market that can have a huge difference between the plain cakes and spectacular ones.

Cake spray paint - now you can spray any color you want to make your cake livelier and fun you can make shape images, lettering and any decoration using a cake spray paint. Its fine mist can create that speckled effect however, do not put the nozzle of the spray too close to the cake's icing or it may cause shirring or dents.

Cake decorating combs - like a big hair comb, the cake decorating combs come in different types of serrated edges and various widths. This comes handy in smoothing a buttercream frosting for easy rolling in fondant. It creates a very flat yet tacky edge which allows the fondant to attach smoothly to your cake. You can also use this comb to create patterns and swirls.

Cake stencils - are available online which is perfect to use in fondant cakes. These cakes have the smoothest surface which is perfect for creating any images. You can also use cake stencils in royal cream and buttercream iced cakes. It si easier now to embossed cake lettering and designs using this product.

Decorating gel - another innovation, the decorating gel is a useful stuff for easy writing of messages and decor in your cake. This is made of pure glycerin and is handier than tinting glycerin yourself. You can also use this to accents or achieve a stained glass effect on your cake.

Edibles - the edible confetti usually composed of rosette and star-shaped candies available in specialty cooking stores or large grocery stores. It is perfect in creating borders or forming a letter. For a more festive look, sprinkle it liberally on top of the cake. We also have the edible glitters that come in rainbow colors. This will look good in combination with stencils and buttercream decorations.

Luster dust - is a fantastic product you can use in decorating fondant. This fine, edible glitter creates n gum paste, sugar shapes and frosting. It is made of a few vodka or gin and some extracts such as lemon and vanilla. There are several colors available that can be applied using a small paint brush or airbrush. You can also use tea strainer to come up with that gleaming effect.

Creative Toppings

If you are a beginner and is not yet comfortable in piping frosting or working with rolled fondant, achieve that creative look with the help of some nuts, cookies, cashew and fresh fruits. Try using ingredients available at home such as pecans, gingersnaps, hazelnuts, pistachios, shredded coconut or cream filled chocolate cookies. Make sure that you will consume your cake with fresh fruits and cookies at least 2 hours after serving it.

Baking Decorations

Baking tools and materials can be very helpful in your cake decoration. You can find it a craft stores, supermarkets and specialty food stores.

Pearl sugar - can add unique texture to the cake.

Nonpareils- are available in single and mixed colors, these balls are same with pearl sugar balls which add appeal to the cake's overall look.

Colored decorating sugar - this is available in fine-grain sanding sugar, sparkle sugar and coarse sugars.

Jimmies - also known as sprinkles, jimmies can be purchased in single or mixed colors.

Coloring the Frosting

If you are familiar with frosting and would like to give it a try, you can choose to have it flavored or tinted. White frosting, butter frosting and cream cheese frosting are good in tint with any flavor and color that will match your cakes flavor.

There are 2 ways on how to add color to your frosting. First, you can use gel or paste food coloring which is highly concentrated. This also comes in different colors which you can find at specialty cooking stores or hobby stores. Add the mixture little by little or until you achieve the right consistency.

Next you can try <u>using liquid food coloring</u> which is normally available in grocery stores. Stir drops of it into your frosting until you come up with your desired hues.

<u>Flavoring the Frosting</u>

Whilst you are free to add flavors in your frosting, make sure that the flavor will complement the taste and appearance of your cake. Almond, maple, vanilla and rum are the most common flavorings which is safe to use.

Being new to cake decorating not only requires you to be creative but to be brave as well. Mixing and matching of decorations is one of the fun part of making cake however, this is the most challenging too. Continue exploring and getting ideas, tips and techniques to enhance your baking and decorating skills.

Chapter 6

Decorating Mistakes to Avoid

Apparently, cake decorating is a fun and wonderful hobby for some of us thus, it attracts more fans and enthusiasts nowadays. However, due to too much enthusiasm and lack of proper guidance and inexperience, not most of us who try this get successful. Hence we will point out some of the mistake beginners commit in their first attempt in baking and decorating cake.

<u>More accessories, less skills</u>

With all the products, ingredients, tools and innovations offered in the cake industry, we tend to buy most of it without actually knowing how to use them accordingly. Moreover, some of us believe that the more accessories they have, the simpler their cake decorating task will become.

For an instance, you can purchase hundreds of various decorating tubes in the market. However buying the full set of tubes will only make it more difficult for you to decorate your cake since there are tons of choices to choose from. Picking up a certain design becomes a difficult task although in fact, it only requires you at least 2 tubes to start. Likewise, seasoned cake decorators use less than 10 tubes in decorating three-tier cakes.

<u>Complex and intricate designs</u>

In the context of cake decorating, one must master the simplest and basic designs and techniques first before trying the complex ones. Being comfortable in creating basic designs will give you an edge when doing the detailed decorations.

Yes, trying fresh ideas and inspirations you found on the internet is a good thing but executing these designs while you are still beginning is a sure shot way to frustrations. Practice with the simple cakes and basic designs before you moved one with other ideas you have in mind.

Incorrect icing preparations

We must know by now that icing is the cake's foundation in terms of decorating. To become successful in whatever designs or patterns you want for your cake, proper icing preparation is crucial. The icing depends on the type of the cake and your decoration depends on the type of icing you will make.

Remember the icing's viscosity is important. As for the rule of the thumb, even the smallest amount of grease can affect the consistency of the icing so make sure that you properly clean the utensils you will use. If use for border work, keep the icing's consistency low to avoid breaking the border. For designs such as flowers however, make the consistency high so the shapes will form accordingly.

Rushing the cake to be done

Every oven varies and some cake recipes take longer to fully baked thus, test the cake first for doneness before taking it out from the oven. You may get excited and take out the cake earlier than it should be. A toothpick or skewer will help you determine if the cake is done.

Similarly, refrain from opening the oven door ahead of the indicated cooking time in the recipe. Cheesecake and flourless cakes tend to collapse upon decorating when the heat of the oven fluctuated as you open its door ahead of the baking time.

We know that waiting seems hard to do especially if we are too much excited to start the decoration process but again, some little restraint will be worth the wait. Let your cake cool slightly after removing it from the oven. Do not replace it in the fridge just to cool it immediately. Rapid cooling will only make the cake stickier or to collapse. Once the cake is properly cooled, start with the frosting, glazing and putting more decorations.

Being aware of these mistakes will make the most of your cake baking and decorating experience fun-filled and awesome. Likewise it will keep you ahead of other newbie decorators. Practice more and soon you will be making sumptuous and eye-catching cakes.

Conclusion

Thank you again for downloading this book!

I hope this book was able to help you to get started in creating wonderful and festive cakes for all occasions.

The next step upon successful completion of this book is to enhance your decorating skills and unleash your potential as a professional baker of not just cakes but other pastries and sweets.

Remember that making cakes need not to be an expensive hobby. With some practice, creativity and resourcefulness, you are sure to come up with cakes like a real pro!

Anyone can put some sprinkles or glitters to their cake but true decoration requires patience and skills. Moreover imagination will make a huge difference.

Explore other ideas, adopt some inspirations and create your own techniques but be sure to master the basic first for a more fun-filled baking and decorating process.

Finally, if you enjoyed this book, please take the time to share your thoughts and post a review on Amazon. It'd be greatly appreciated!

Thank you and good luck!

Bonus Chapter: 5 Mug Recipes

First Five Mug Recipes You Can Make in Minutes

A. Cake Mug Recipes

Here are some delicious cake mug recipes which will take barely thirty minutes to prepare:

i) Chocolate cookie mug cake

The ingredients you need for this mug cake include:

- Egg – 1

- Brown sugar – 3 tablespoons

- Wheat flour – ⅓ cup

- Soft butter – 1 tablespoon

- Tiny chocolate chips – 3 tablespoons

How to go about the preparation:

- o Crack your egg and pour it in your mug

- o Next, add the brown sugar in the same mug and mix the two.

- o Then add the flour and continue mixing your ingredients.

- o Next, add the butter and mix it as evenly as you can.

- o Add the chocolate chips as well

- o Now use a spoon to mix all those ingredients properly.

- Once you are satisfied that all your ingredients are well mixed, put the mug in your microwave just the way it is with its ingredients.

- Switch on your microwave and set the timer at one and a half (1½) minutes. You could even put it at a full two minutes. How fast is that!

And now, all you need on the side is some ice cream and you are full and happy.

ii) Pumpkin mug cake

Here are the ingredients:

- •Egg – 1

- •Skim milk – 2 tablespoons

- •Vanilla extract (pure) - ¼ teaspoon

- •Pumpkin puree – ¼ cup

- •Wheat flour – 7 tablespoons

- •Brown sugar – ¼ cup

- Ground cinnamon – ¼ teaspoon

- Mixed spices – ¼ teaspoon

- Kosher salt – ¼ teaspoon

How to go about making the pumpkin mug cake:

- Put all your ingredients in a medium sized bowl and mix well.

- Once you are satisfied with your mixing, pour your mixture into your chosen mug.

- Put the mug into the microwave.

- Set the microwave to 1½ minutes at a high temperature.

- After that time is up, open the microwave to check your mug. If you find spillage, wipe the mess off the mug and re-set your microwave to another 1½ minutes and switch on.

- Once that time is up, take a few nuts and some whipped cream and use them to garnish your pumpkin mug cake.

iii)   Mug Brownie without gluten

Here are your gluten-free ingredients:

- Oat flour = ¼ cup

You can also substitute this with quinoa flour

- Brown sugar = ¼ cup

- Cocoa powder = 2 tablespoons

Note that this cocoa powder should not be sweetened.

- Salt = Just a pinch

- Vegetable oil = 2 tablespoons

- Milk = 2 tablespoons

You can always use water in place of milk here.

How to go about making the Mug Brownie:

- Mix all your dry ingredients in your chosen mug.

- Ensure that all the ingredients are evenly spread.

- Then add the oil and the milk or water and continue to stir and mix till everything is well distributed.

- Now put the mug containing your mixture in the microwave.

- Turn on the microwave on high and set the timer to 30 seconds.

- If you do not get a springy top the way the brownie needs to be, keep the mug in there for another 30 seconds.

- When you find your brownie a bit sticky but springy on top, remove it from the microwave.

This Mug Brownie is best when still warm.

It is interesting to note that none of the above mug recipes even hits five minutes in the microwave. That essentially means that most of your time is spent in preparing your ingredients. How much time do you really need to prepare your ingredients, most of which are ready-to-eat in the first place? You can now see why it is possible to have mug recipes conveniently ready in as little as ten minutes.

iv) Mug Cake of Peanut Butter and Chocolate

This is a delicious filling cake that takes just a couple of minutes to get ready. Here are its ingredients:

- Egg – 1

- Brown sugar – 1 tablespoon

- Peanut butter – 2 tablespoons

- Flour – 1 tablespoon

- Cocoa – 1 tablespoon

- Baking Powder – ¼ tablespoon

- Chocolate chips – a handful

Here is how to go about preparing this delicious cake:

- Get a bowl and beat your egg in it.

- Then add the brown sugar and stir well.

- Now add the baking powder followed with the cocoa, flour and peanut butter.

- Ensure you mix everything properly so that each ingredient is well distributed.

- Now grease your mug.

- Pour your well mixed ingredients into your greased mug.

- Now put your mug in the microwave.

- Set the microwave timer to one (1) minute.

- Your work is done and your mug cake of peanut butter and chocolate is ready for consumption. In fact, you do not need to shift your cake anywhere else – you can just eat it directly from that mug you used for preparation.

B.   Whole Grain Meal

v) Mug of Macaroni and Cheese

This is one healthy and delicious meal in a mug. It takes a short while to cook, only that you will need to keep checking it in interludes of a minute or so.

Here are the requisite ingredients:

- Whole grain macaroni – ⅓ cup

- Water – ¼ cup

- Shredded cheddar cheese – ⅓ cup

- Milk – 2 teaspoons

Of course you will need a large mug to cook from.

How to go about preparing this whole meal:

   o Put the macaroni in your large mug.

   o Add all the water. In fact, in case you have a very strong microwave, you may wish to add the water so that it gets to half a cup.

      But instead of going that way, it is advisable to stick to the given measurement, then if you find the macaroni drying up prematurely, you add some tablespoons of water; something that you can do gradually.

   o Now put your contents in the microwave and switch it on.

   o When it comes to cooking time, you need to target six (6) minutes. But since you need to check your macaroni from time to time, you could begin by setting four (4) minutes, after which you take the time to stir your macaroni.

   o Resume the cooking and then stir it after two (2) minutes.

   o Finally, return your mug to the microwave for the final cooking minute.

   o Remove your mug from the microwave and ignore that little water you see at the bottom.

   o Now add all your cheese on top of your ready pasta.

- Return the mug to the microwave and set the timer to 30 seconds. In case your microwave is not one of the strongest, you could set its timer to 45 seconds. The whole idea is to melt your cheese so that it begins to seep into the pasta.

- Remove the mug from the microwave and stir the contents.

- Finally, sprinkle the milk on the contents.

You are now ready to have your fill and keep yourself healthy in the process. And, obviously, you have not spent anything close to half an hour!

Made in the USA
Middletown, DE
05 June 2024